THE SECRET WORLD OF

Crabs

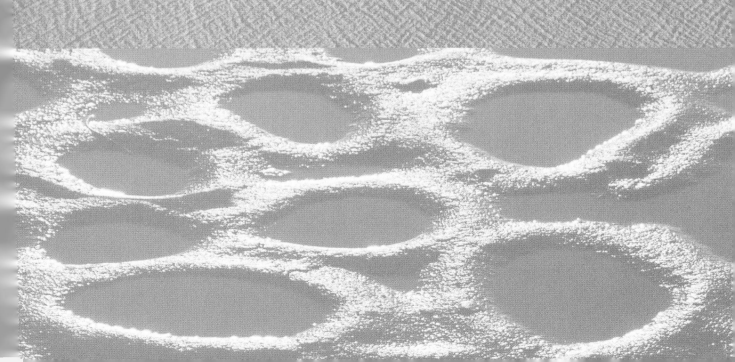

THE SECRET WORLD OF
Crabs

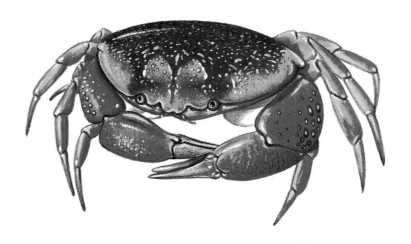

Theresa Greenaway

www.raintreepublishers.co.uk
Visit our website to find out more information about **Raintree** books.

To order:
 Phone 44 (0) 1865 888112
 Send a fax to 44 (0) 1865 314091
 Visit the Raintree Bookshop at www.raintreepublishers.co.uk to browse our catalogue and order online.

First published in Great Britain by Raintree,
Halley Court, Jordan Hill, Oxford
OX2 8EJ, part of Harcourt Education.
Raintree is a registered trademark of Harcourt Education Ltd.

Produced for Raintree by Discovery Books
Editors: Helen Dwyer and Catherine Clarke
Series Consultant: Michael Chinery
Design: Ian Winton
Illustrations: Stuart Lafford
Production: Jonathan Smith

Originated by Dot Gradations Ltd
Printed and bound in China by South China Printing Company

ISBN 1 844 21589 X
07 06 05 04 03
10 9 8 7 6 5 4 3 2 1

British Library Cataloguing in Publication Data
Greenaway, Theresa
The Secret World of Crabs
595.3'86
A full catalogue record for this book is available from the British Library.

Acknowledgements
The publishers would like to thank the following for permission to reproduce photographs:
Bruce Coleman Collection pp. 8 (Orion Press), 10 (Jeff Foott), 12, 14 (John Cancalosi), 16 (Kevin Cullimore), 19 (Jane Burton), 28 (Andrew Purcell), 30 (Jane Burton), 38 (John Cancalosi), 39 (Jeff Foott), 40 (Mary Plage.), 42 (Andrew Davies); Natural History Photographic Agency pp. 11 & 13 (B.Jones & M.Shimlock), 15 top (A.N.T.), 24 (Karl Switak), 26 (Anthony Bannister), 34 & 35 (B.Jones & M.Shimlock), 36 (Yves Lanceau); Oxford Scientific Films pp. 9 & 15 bottom (G.I.Bernard), 20 (Paul Kay), 21 (Animals Animals), 25 (Richard Herrman), 27 (John Pontier/Animals Animals), 37 (Karen Gowlett-Holmes), 41 (Mark Deeble & Victoria Stone); Premaphotos pp. 17, 22 & 23 (K.G.Preston-Mafham), 32 & 43 (Dr Rod Preston-Mafham)
All background images © Steck-Vaughn Collection (Corbis Royalty Free, Getty Royalty Free, and StockBYTE).

Cover photograph reproduced with permission of the Natural History Photographic Agency (Bill Coster).

Every effort has been made to contact copyright holders of any material reproduced in this book. Any omissions will be rectified in subsequent printings if notice is given to the publishers.

Any words appearing in the text in bold, **like this**, are explained in the Glossary.

Contents

Curious crabs

 The largest crab is the giant spider crab from Japan. Its chelipeds span 3.6 metres, and its body is about 40 centimetres across.

 The heaviest crab is a fully grown giant crab from the sea near southern Australia. Its body is about 43 centimetres across, and it weighs 12.4 kilograms. Out of water, its claws are too heavy for it to lift.

 The sand-dollar pea crab is one of the smallest crabs. Its tiny body only reaches 5 millimetres in length.

 The horseshoe crab is not a crab at all. It is much more closely related to spiders and scorpions.

Crabs belong to a group of animals called **crustaceans**. Their closest relatives are shrimps, prawns and lobsters. Like insects and spiders, crustaceans are **arthropods**. All arthropods have a hard body covering, or **exoskeleton**, and several pairs of jointed legs. It is easy to recognize a crab. It has a short body that is often wider than it is long and two big pairs of **pincers**, or claws, held out in front.

A crab's body has a head, **thorax**, and **abdomen**. The head and thorax are joined together under a hard shell called a **carapace**. Crabs have five pairs of legs attached to the thorax. The two front legs, called **chelipeds**, each have a pair of pincers. Behind these are four pairs of walking legs, each with a pointed foot. At the back of the thorax is the crab's abdomen, which is no more than a small flap in most crabs.

There are more than 4500 different **species**, or kinds, of crab. They are divided into two groups, a large group of true crabs and a smaller group containing hermit crabs, porcelain crabs and king crabs. True crabs have small, flat abdomens that are folded up against the underside of the thorax. There are no tail-like flaps at the tip of this abdomen. Hermit, porcelain and king crabs do have tail flaps. Although the abdomens of porcelain and king crabs fold flat against the thorax, hermit crabs have long, unfolded abdomens and live inside the empty shells of sea snails.

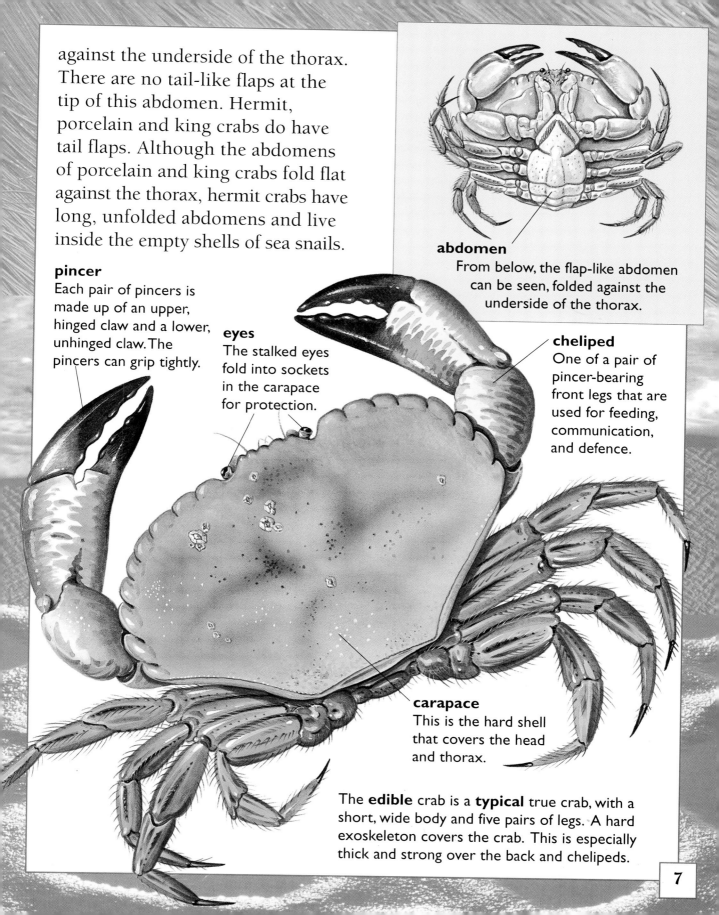

abdomen
From below, the flap-like abdomen can be seen, folded against the underside of the thorax.

pincer
Each pair of pincers is made up of an upper, hinged claw and a lower, unhinged claw. The pincers can grip tightly.

eyes
The stalked eyes fold into sockets in the carapace for protection.

cheliped
One of a pair of pincer-bearing front legs that are used for feeding, communication, and defence.

carapace
This is the hard shell that covers the head and thorax.

The **edible** crab is a **typical** true crab, with a short, wide body and five pairs of legs. A hard exoskeleton covers the crab. This is especially thick and strong over the back and chelipeds.

Most crabs live in the sea, from the **shoreline** down to the deepest parts of the ocean. Shoreline crabs are covered by salty water or open to the air as the **tides** come in and go out. Storms may send huge waves crashing down, so crabs and other shoreline wildlife must be able to cling to rocks or take shelter. In deep water, the conditions are calmer, but there may be fewer places to hide.

▲ In spite of its very long, thin legs, the giant spider crab walks quite slowly over the seabed.

Some other kinds of crabs, like the Chinese mitten crab, for example, live in fresh water.

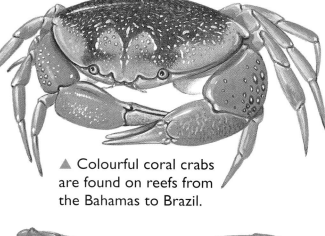

▲ Colourful coral crabs are found on reefs from the Bahamas to Brazil.

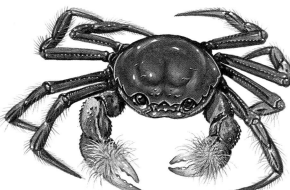

▲ An adult Chinese mitten crab lives in freshwater rivers but has to travel to the mouth of the river to **mate**.

Others spend part of the day on land, and some, such as the mangrove crab and the soldier crab, spend most of their time on land. To avoid drying out, land crabs hide somewhere damp during the hottest part of the day.

▲ The **tropical** land crab digs down in damp soil and makes a hole in which to spend the day.

HEAD

At the front of a crab's head there is a pair of eyes on stalks. Slightly below these are two pairs of feelers, or **antennae**. The crab's mouth lies below these. The mouth of a crab is made up of pairs of hard mouthparts, which have different uses. A pair of jaws hold the food. Other parts pull bits off and put them into the crab's mouth. A flap on one pair of these mouthparts pumps water over the crab's **gills**, so the crab can breathe.

Hard mouthparts process the crab's food before it is finally swallowed.

CRAB SHELL

The whole body of a true crab is covered and enclosed by a hard outer layer of **cuticle** called an **exoskeleton**. This layer is made of **protein** and a chalky material. The cuticle covering the crab's back and its **chelipeds** is especially thick. This hard, shelly outer layer protects the crab from wear and tear and also helps to protect it from **predators**. Thinner, more flexible cuticle covers the joints of the legs, so that they can bend. A crab's hard shell cannot stretch so, in order to grow, the old shell is sometimes shed. This is called **moulting**.

A crab's hard shell also contains substances called pigments that give each **species** its colour and pattern. The light-coloured markings on the carapace of this lined shore crab help to **identify** it.

Hermit crabs

A hermit crab has a hard layer of cuticle covering the front part of its body and its legs, but its long **abdomen** is soft. Hermit crabs live inside the empty shells of other animals, usually those of periwinkles, whelks and other sea snails. The curved abdomen fits snugly inside a coiled snail shell, and the two tiny tail flaps grip the tip of the shell firmly. A hermit crab also grips the rim of its shell with its back two pairs of walking legs. When a hermit crab grows too big for its shell, it has to find a larger one.

BREATHING

All animals need **oxygen** to breathe. Land crabs breathe air, but most crabs can breathe only in water. Delicate, feathery **gills** on each side of the **thorax** take in oxygen dissolved in the water. The gills are hidden in a chamber (space) under the sides of the **carapace**. Water enters the gill chamber through tiny holes between the legs. It washes over the gills and then leaves through openings just above the mouth. Fiddler crabs store water so that they can breathe when on land.

Crabs in motion

 Ghost crabs can run forwards, backwards and sideways at speeds of up to 6.4 kilometres (4 miles) per hour.

 The mangrove tree crab climbs 10 metres or more to the tops of mangrove trees.

 The large land crab digs a 1-metre- deep burrow 10 centimetres across, with a small space at the bottom where the crab can keep cool and damp during the day.

 The mud crab digs a burrow with an emergency exit. Its U-shaped burrow has two main entrances and sometimes side tunnels as well.

Why do crabs walk sideways? There is a very good reason for this – the long walking legs are so close together on each side of a crab's short body that if it were to move forwards, the legs would trip over each other. By scuttling sideways, this is avoided. Many kinds of crabs, such as the Sally Lightfoot, can sprint over sand or rocky ground extremely quickly. Crabs can walk on land as well as over the seabed or underwater rocks.

As well as walking on land or under the water, some kinds of crabs use their legs to burrow into the ground under the seabed, and some are surprisingly good at climbing. How they normally get from place to

Like other crab sprinters that need to move quickly across open spaces, this Sally Lightfoot crab has large eyes to **detect predators**.

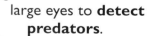

place depends mainly on where they live. Many kinds of crabs live on rocky shores. Those such as the king crab are slow-moving crabs with a thick, heavy shell and large, powerful **pincers**. Their short legs allow them to cling tightly to rocks and to pull themselves through seaweed or into sheltered rock **crevices**. Crabs that live in open places with little shelter, such as muddy or sandy beaches, are sprinters. Ghost and fiddler crabs need to be able to run quickly back to their burrows when danger threatens.

SKILFUL SWIMMERS

Most crabs are able to push themselves through water, but the

Swimming crabs are flattened and have a light carapace to help them move speedily through the water. The shell of this swimming crab is covered with tiny sea animals called hydroids.

swimming crabs are excellent swimmers. These crabs need to be able to swim quickly to catch the fast-moving fish they eat. They have large eyes to help them see their **prey**. Swimming crabs are made for speed, with light shells and thin legs. The back pair of legs is flattened into paddles that can be used both to move the crab forwards and to send it darting sideways through the water. The **carapace** of the blue crab has long spines on each side, which help it to swim sideways.

CLIMBING CRABS

Most crabs can clamber over rocks and underwater **debris**, but some can climb over beds of waving seaweed or large **reefs**. Spider crabs and coral crabs are strong climbers with feet that can grip tightly, so that even strong waves do not dislodge them. On land, crabs such as the rocky shore crab and the mangrove tree crab also have feet that help them keep a grip on trees and branches.

sideways. Back-burrowing crabs, such as mole crabs, sit on the sand, lean backwards, then dig into the sand with their legs until only their eyes or **antennae** can be seen. Some of these burrowers are able to dig very quickly and make a new burrow every time they need to hide.

This crab keeps a firm hold on the tree trunk by pushing its feet into cracks in the bark.

BURROWING

The only place to shelter on a sandy seabed or beach is under the sand or mud itself. Burrowing crabs either burrow backwards or

Crabs that live partly or completely on land, such as fiddler, ghost and mud crabs, dig more long-lasting burrows. These may be just simple upright tunnels of about 15 centimetres or they may be more complicated, branching burrows. These crabs are side-burrowers.

Robber crab

The robber crab (also known as the coconut crab) of the South Pacific and Indian oceans is well known for its habit of stealing anything that takes its fancy. People watching have been amused by robber crabs making off with items such as cans, watches, sandals and cutlery! Robber crabs are also excellent climbers. They can climb 20 metres or so up a smooth palm tree trunk to feast on its fruit.

Using the legs on one side of its body, the crab digs out soil or mud and carries it in balls to the entrance. These burrows last for many weeks. The crabs shelter in them when the tide comes in or whenever they are threatened. They plug the entrances with a mud lid.

The ghost crab races back to its burrow at the slightest chance of danger. Its long-stalked eyes fold sideways into its shell when it is safely underground.

15

Crab senses

Crabs have senses of sight, touch, taste and smell. They can also **detect vibrations** in water, and some can also detect vibrations passing through the ground. Some kinds of crabs, including ghost and fiddler crabs, can hear. A crab's senses help it to know what to do and when. They help it to detect **predators** so that it can escape from danger and help it to find food, a **mate** and a place to live.

The velvet swimming crab lives among rocks in shallow waters near the shore. By day it shelters in a rock **crevice**, but when it senses increasing darkness, it comes out to feed.

 Ghost crabs have the best eyesight – they can see a large moving object from about 100 metres away.

 A crab uses its senses of smell, taste and touch to find food under the water.

 Tiny sense organs at the bottom of each antenna let the crab know which way is up and help it to keep its balance in air or water.

 A ghost crab's eyes are wrapped right around its eyestalks, so the crab can see in every direction.

A crab's senses also tell it when the time is right to come out of its shelter, and when to return. In the sea, most crabs are active at night. Swimming crabs, walking crabs and spider crabs all come out at night to feed. As day breaks, these crabs return to shelters under rocks or in burrows.

Shore crab behaviour also depends on the **tides**. The common shore crab, or green crab, comes out to feed at high tide when the shore is covered by water. When the tide goes out, it hides in rock pools or under seaweed. It sometimes appears at high tide during the day, but is most active at high tide at night. Fiddler and ghost crabs hide when the tide is in and only appear as it goes out. Many of these kinds of crabs are most active during daytime low tides.

EYES

Crabs' eyes are on the tips of stalks, and they fold into sockets in the **carapace** for protection. Having eyes on stalks means that even a flat crab has a good view of its surroundings. Crabs have compound eyes, just like insects.

A ghost crab uses its eyes to spot moving **prey** as well as larger predators but it relies on its sense of smell to discover other food items such as carrion (dead animals).

This means that each eye is made up of thousands of small units, each with its own tiny lens. Compound eyes do not give a clear image but are very sensitive to movement and can see colours. Eyesight varies from **species** to species, and it is less important to some kinds of crabs than others. Thick-shelled shore crabs rely on their strength rather than sight and therefore have small eyes.

Life in the deep

The deep sea crab lives at about 2500 metres in warm water vents (chimney-like structures) in the eastern Pacific Ocean. It is completely dark at this depth, so this crab is totally blind. It finds its **prey** of worms and deep-sea clams by smell and the vibrations these animals make in the darkness.

A SENSE OF TOUCH

Despite their hard shell, crabs have a good sense of touch. This is because growing through the **cuticle** are tiny but very sensitive bristles. These touch-sensitive bristles are scattered all over a crab's body, and there are many of them on the legs and feet. Other types of hairs are sensitive to **vibrations** travelling through the water. These hairs are found mostly along the **pincers**.

CAN CRABS HEAR?

It is not yet known whether all crabs can hear, but scientists have discovered that ghost and fiddler crabs certainly can. These crabs make special sounds to attract **mates** or warn off other crabs. Some sounds are made as the crabs rub their legs. They make other sounds by tapping the mud or sand with their pincers. To **detect** these sounds, the crabs have 'ears' inside the tips of their legs. These are small, flat sheets of cuticle that work a bit like the eardrum in each of our ears.

TASTE AND SMELL

Crabs can smell things to eat underwater by sensing **chemicals** from food with the tufts of hairs on the tips of their **antennae**. When a crab detects these chemicals, it starts to search for the food by moving in the direction where the smell is strongest. Taste-sensitive hairs are located on the mouthparts, along the pincers and on the crab's feet. When the feet touch something **edible**, these hairs tell the crab to pick it up with its claws and start eating.

Different kinds of hairs and bristles on a crab's antennae, mouthparts, pincers and the rest of its legs are sensitive to touch, taste and smell, so a crab can find food even in the dark.

Food and feeding

Most crabs are happy to eat almost anything, plant or animal, dead or alive, that they come across. Animals that have such a wide range of food items in their diet are called **omnivores**. Crabs like these will hardly ever go hungry. They will always manage to find something to eat. Other crabs are more fussy in their eating habits, but even so, in times of need, they too will eat whatever is available.

Predatory crabs use their **pincers** to catch their **prey**, and all omnivorous crabs catch or search for their food and pick it up with their pincers. Each pair of pincers is made up of an upper, hinged claw and a lower, unhinged claw.

A hungry shore crab will catch and eat another crab if it can overcome it, and it will also eat dead crabs.

 A pair of trainers belonging to a scientist studying crabs on Christmas Island were snipped, shredded and then carried away by a robber crab!

 Robber crabs snip their way through the hard shells of coconuts and feed on the white coconut inside.

 Mangrove crabs will try to eat anything – they will even sneak up to a rat and grab its tail!

 Land crabs eat mostly plants but will eat a dead animal if they get the chance.

 Freshwater crabs add fish and frogs to their menu when they can catch them.

A dead fish is an easy meal for a crab. This Sally Lightfoot crab is snipping off pieces of flesh with its pincers and passing them to its mouthparts.

The hinge allows the upper claw to move to and fro so that it can grip. The jointed parts of the rest of the **cheliped** allow the crab to reach in all directions with its claws.

The shape and size of these claws vary from **species** to species. Most have saw-like teeth along the edge of one or both claws. These help the crab to grip its food, and in some species, such as robber crabs, these teeth are sharp enough to cut up hard food such as coconuts. Most crabs use their claws to pull apart their food and pass pieces of it to their jaws.

These jaws hold on to and bite the food, so that the next sets of mouthparts can shred it and pass it into the crab's mouth.

PREDATORY CRABS

Swimming crabs are able to catch fast-moving fish or prawns because they can dart through the water quickly and snatch their **prey** using their thin, sharply toothed claws. Heavier crabs, such as the **edible** crab, cannot catch such active prey. These crabs are mostly carnivorous (flesh-eating), feeding on worms, slow-moving starfish and **molluscs**, such as mussels, the shells of which they crush with their strong pincers. They also use their pincers to dig their prey out of the sand.

SCAVENGERS

When the **tide** goes out, it leaves a line of **debris** along the shore. The debris includes strands of dead seaweed, dead seabirds, dead fish, pieces of wood and all kinds of rubbish that has either been thrown from ships or washed down rivers and into the sea. Tiny **invertebrates** such as sand hoppers and small flies swarm all over it. Crabs and other animals search among this debris for food – a way of feeding called **scavenging**.

These land hermit crabs are scavengers, feeding on anything **edible** that they come across. Here, they are eating the debris that collects in the cracks in a piece of driftwood.

FILTER FEEDING

The action of waves helps to break up dead animals and dead seaweed. The larger pieces sink, but the smaller ones float. Sea water carries much smaller living creatures as well. Animals that get their food by straining these tiny creatures from the water are known as filter feeders.

A few crabs get their food in this way. The mole crab has feathery **antennae** that trap tiny pieces of food from the water. These are collected together by the **pincers** into a ball of food, which is then put into the mole crab's mouth.

Food from mud

The fiddler crab and the sand-bubbler crab (pictured here) leave their burrows to feed when the tide goes out. On the open shore, the crabs scoop mud or sand into their mouths with their claws. There, the mouthparts separate out pieces of plants and animals, and spit out what cannot be eaten.

SCRAPING A MEAL

Underwater rocks and corals are covered with a layer of tiny sea creatures. The pincers of spider crabs, such as the red spider crab, end in ridged, spoon-like tips that are used to scrape off this **nutritious** layer. The mouthparts are hairy, to prevent the crabs from dropping these small pieces of food.

Competitive crabs

 Up to 500,000 young king crabs cluster together to make gigantic heaps on the seabed.

 Crabs that start a quarrel are usually larger than their opponent and therefore more likely to win.

 A blue crab shows that it has been beaten in a fight by folding its claws close against its body and crouching low on the ground.

 In a fight, river crabs lock pincers and push against each other. The winner is the crab that overturns its opponent.

Crabs of the same kind often live close to each other, but competition for food means that each has its own patch of **territory** to defend. Actual fighting is very risky, because an injured crab is more likely to be caught by a **predator**, so signals are usually used to solve these quarrels. If this fails and a neighbour comes too close, a fight may follow. Legs may be lost during fights, or the protective **carapace** cracked. Smaller crabs are even killed – and eaten by the winner!

These Sally Lightfoot crabs are fighting, trying to damage each other with their pincers. Unless one backs down, even the winner may suffer a serious injury.

Land crabs may gather together in large 'armies' while they are searching for food. When the young adult land crabs first come out from the sea, larger adults are often waiting to eat them!

crabs are most often males, and they are allowed to go where they want, even into the territory of other crabs. A smaller male or female will not risk injury or death by challenging a larger crab.

SIGNALS

If two crabs meet face-to-face, then the smaller crab usually backs off rather than risk injury. If two well-matched crabs meet up, things are carried a stage further. The two crabs start to signal to each other by raising a pair of walking legs. Sometimes a signalling crab raises itself up on to its feet in order to make itself look larger and more fierce. The next stage is more aggressive. Each waves its **chelipeds**. If this exchange of signals does not sort out which crab is the winner, then the crabs start to push or barge into each other and may take hold of each other with their **pincers**. Even then, one crab usually backs off before any damage is done.

Some kinds of crabs look for safety in numbers, so they get together in large groups. The idea is that if you are the only crab around, a crab-eating predator will surely get you, but if you are one of hundreds of crabs, then there is a good chance that your neighbour will be eaten, and not you!

Some crab **species** even have a system in which some crabs are more important than others. This is usually decided by size and strength. The largest, strongest

TERRITORY

Many of the crabs that spend some or most of their time on land have a **territory** that each defends against intruders. These crabs need a burrow in which to shelter and keep cool. Often the patch of ground surrounding their burrow is where they search for food. An intruder would therefore be a threat to both their home and their food supply.

This mud crab is sending a very clear message. With its **chelipeds** outstretched and claws open, it is threatening an attack if the intruder approaches more closely.

LOOKING AFTER EACH OTHER

Crabs are at risk from **predators**, especially when they are small or when they have just **moulted**. Half-grown crabs of some sea-living **species** gather together in enormous heaps. Spider crabs make heaps with the smaller crabs, surrounded by large, male crabs.

Waving

Male fiddler crabs have one pair of pincers that is much bigger than the other, and usually brightly coloured.
This is so enormous it is no use for feeding. Instead, the male fiddler crab uses it to send signals to all the other fiddler crabs on the **tropical**, **tidal mudflats** where they live.
At low **tide**, as the crabs wander around feeding, each male waves his huge pair of pincers. He does this to show ownership of his territory, to threaten intruders and to attract females.

This is thought to protect females and young crabs from predators such as octopuses or lobsters. Young Alaskan king crabs also pile up on top of each other. Then they spread out into a huge army of crabs that look for food together on the seabed.

Reproduction

 Male crabs are often bigger and have larger claws than females.

 A female crab carrying her eggs is said to be 'in berry'.

 The edible crab lays up to 3 million eggs in a batch!

 A freshly laid crab's egg is tiny – most are about 0.3 millimetres across, but they do become a little bit larger as they develop.

 When a land crab's eggs are about to hatch, the female has to walk back to the sea to let them go.

Male and female crabs have to stop themselves from fighting each other if they are to pair up and **mate**. When a female crab is ready to mate, she gives out signals that the male crab can recognize. Female crabs that live in the water often produce special **chemicals** that males sense and follow. When they meet, a male and female may use special signs or touch each other with their **antennae** to let each other know that they are not going to attack.

Swimming crabs mate just after the female has **moulted**. This velvet swimming crab male will hold on to his mate until her new shell has hardened.

THE MALE AND FEMALE BLUE CRAB

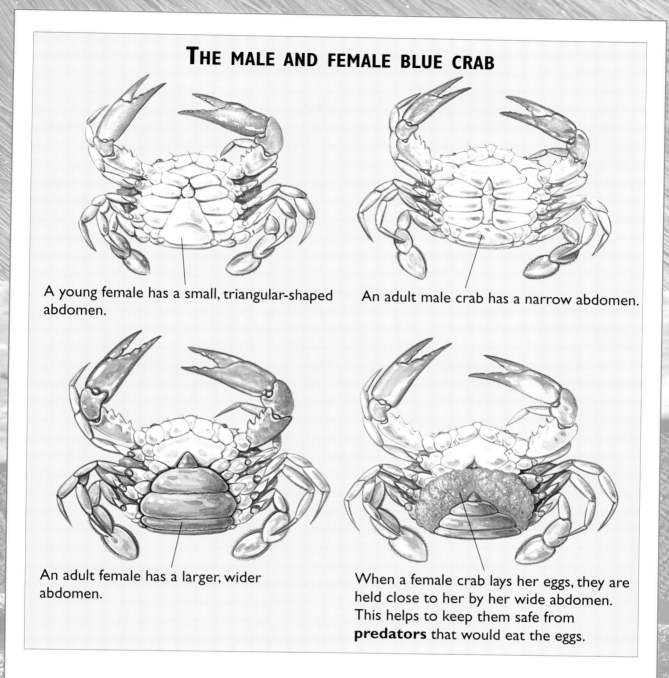

A young female has a small, triangular-shaped abdomen.

An adult male crab has a narrow abdomen.

An adult female has a larger, wider abdomen.

When a female crab lays her eggs, they are held close to her by her wide abdomen. This helps to keep them safe from **predators** that would eat the eggs.

A female crab has a wider **abdomen** than the male, and it is fringed with eight small limb-like structures. After she has mated, eggs develop inside her body until they are ready to be laid in one egg mass. She holds this mass of eggs under her body, kept in place by her flap-like abdomen and gripped by the tiny limbs, until they are ready to hatch. Some crabs may produce two batches of eggs a year, others up to six. Each batch contains thousands of tiny eggs.

COURTING

The male crabs of some **species** do not make very caring **mates** and have the shortest of courtships. A female hermit crab is quickly grabbed by her male mate. If the male spots a larger female hermit crab, however, he will leave the smaller one, because a larger female will be able to produce and carry more eggs.

In comparison, other male crabs seem to be more caring. Male burrowing crabs, shore crabs and some swimming crabs carry the female around for a few days before **mating**. They mate just after the female has **moulted**. The male then continues to carry her around

This female shore crab is in berry (see page 28) and will carry her eggs around for between 12 and 18 weeks until they hatch.

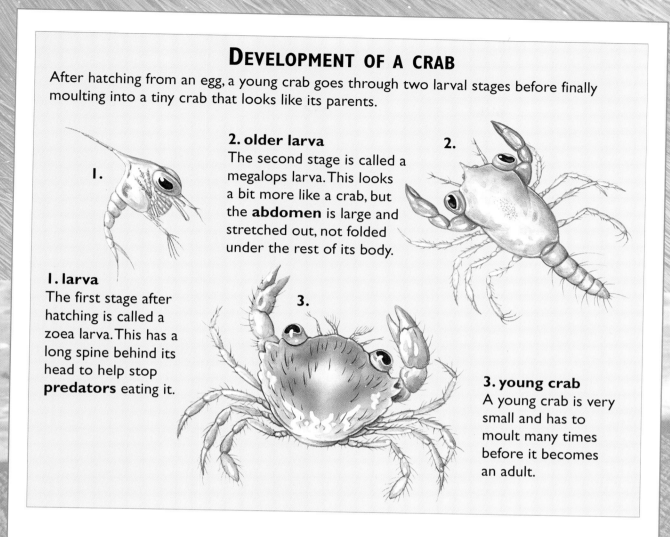

DEVELOPMENT OF A CRAB

After hatching from an egg, a young crab goes through two larval stages before finally moulting into a tiny crab that looks like its parents.

1.

1. larva
The first stage after hatching is called a zoea larva. This has a long spine behind its head to help stop **predators** eating it.

2. older larva
The second stage is called a megalops larva. This looks a bit more like a crab, but the **abdomen** is large and stretched out, not folded under the rest of its body.

2.

3.

3. young crab
A young crab is very small and has to moult many times before it becomes an adult.

and protect her until her new shell has hardened. This stops other males from mating with her.

HATCHING

Most young crabs do not look at all like their parents. They hatch out as tiny **larvae** that mostly live among groups of other tiny animals in the sea, swimming near the surface and feeding on even smaller living creatures. At first, the larva looks a little bit like a tiny shrimp. They do not have any claw-bearing **chelipeds** or walking legs. After two to four moults, they enter a new stage. This older larva has chelipeds and walking legs, but it looks more like a tiny lobster than a crab. It soon sinks to the seabed, where it walks about for a while before finally moulting into a tiny young crab. It will usually be many weeks before a newly hatched larva finally becomes a tiny crab.

MOULTING

The crab's hard **cuticle** does not stretch, so from time to time, a crab has to **moult** in order to grow larger. Young crabs moult more often than older crabs. Because they are soft and helpless for some days after moulting, this is a very dangerous time in the life of a crab, so it hides away somewhere safe.

During moulting, the old cuticle splits along a line under each side of the **carapace**, and the crab wriggles out backwards, pulling its

This shore crab has recently moulted. Its old shell is left lying beside it. The crab has almost doubled in size.

legs out of the old cuticle. The new cuticle is very soft. The crab cannot walk because its legs will not support its weight, and it cannot eat. The crab takes in water and expands, stretching its new skin. After about 32–60 hours, the crab is able to walk, but it may be another 3–7 days before it starts to eat again. The new shell of a large crab may take several weeks to become as hard as the old one.

LOSS OF A LIMB

Limbs may be bitten off in a fight with another crab, or while a crab is trying to escape from a **predator**. Some crabs may actually shed a limb if it is grasped. When a limb is lost or shed, a new one starts to grow almost immediately as a tiny bud. As it regrows, it triggers moulting. After two moults, the new limb will be as large as the original one.

Bromeliad crab

Bromeliads are plants of the pineapple family. They grow in **tropical** South American rainforests, where many kinds perch on the boughs of the tall, rainforest trees. The bases of their large, stiff leaves wrap around each other to make a trap for rainwater. High up in the tree tops, the tiny bromeliad crab lives in these 'tanks' of water, where the female lays up to 100 large, yolky eggs. After they hatch, young crabs develop from the **larvae** after only six days.

I DIDN'T KNOW THAT

33

Self-defence

With a good pair of **pincers** on each **cheliped**, crabs already have handy weapons with which to fight off **predators**, including humans! A crab's claws can pinch really hard and be very painful. You have to be very careful how you pick up a crab, especially a powerful one, such as the **edible** crab. A mangrove crab has another trick to play. It pinches its attacker and then sheds its cheliped, which does not let go. While the victim tries to remove the painful pincer, the crab scuttles away and escapes.

 When porcelain crabs shed pincers they carry on snapping!

 A king crab relies on its shell and strength to protect it from predators.

 When danger threatens, a hermit crab moves back into its shell and blocks the entrance with its right claw, which is larger than the left claw.

 The common hermit crab puts as many as three stinging Calliactis anemones on its shell to protect itself.

 To see in the dark, deep-sea hermit crabs carry anemones that can give off light!

The boxer crab holds a sea **anemone** in each claw. It uses these as stinging weapons when danger threatens, by waving the anemones at the predator.

Like a zebra, Adam's urchin crab has black and white stripes. It lives among the long striped spines of a poisonous sea urchin, where its stripes make it hard to see.

Many animals find crabs so tasty that they have learned how to avoid the pincers, so crabs have developed other ways of defending themselves. Some simply rely on not being noticed by a hungry predator. They are coloured or patterned to match their background. Others have formed curious, but fascinating, partnerships with very different kinds of sea animals. In many cases, both partners benefit from this teamwork. In others the relationship seems a bit one-sided.

CAMOUFLAGE

Many crabs blend in perfectly with their background. This kind of disguise is called camouflage. As long as they keep still, it can be difficult to make out their shape. Hairy wharf crabs have tufts of hairs on their legs and back. These crabs live on the seabed, where sand and silt gets trapped among their tufts, making them look just like sandy pebbles.

Others take camouflage a step further. Spider crabs plant pieces of seaweed and sponges among the hooked hairs on their rough **carapaces**, and some pieces settle there naturally. This makes a spider crab look just like a seaweed-covered rock, but the spider crab has to replace its camouflage every time it **moults**. Sponge crabs search around for the sea-orange sponge. They break off a small piece of this sponge and hold it against their carapace with their back pair of walking legs. This sponge grows right over the crab's carapace in an orange-yellow dome. Tucked away underneath, the crab is completely out of sight.

CURIOUS PARTNERSHIPS

There are many partnerships between sea **anemones** and crabs. The crabs are helped, partly because the anemones disguise the crabs, and partly because the sea anemones have nasty stings that help to keep **predators** away. The anemones are helped because they feed on pieces of food stirred up from the seabed as the crab moves around.

This hermit crab has two stinging anemones on its shell. They protect the crab from predators. The anemones feed on pieces of food from the hermit crab's **prey** and also from the seabed as the crab walks around.

The cloak anemone lives with a small hermit crab that is only about 5 centimetres long when it is fully grown. When the crab is young, it is small enough to live inside a winkle shell. Instead of perching on the top of the shell, the cloak anemone settles underneath. It grows up and right over the winkle shell, completely covering it. Then it grows out over the opening, to make a tube. The hermit crab and the anemone grow larger together, so the crab never needs to find a bigger home in which to live.

Pea crabs

Tiny pea crabs protect themselves by living inside the shell of a living **mollusc**, such as a mussel. The pea crab gets a safe home inside the thick shell of the mollusc, and it gets something else as well – a food supply. Molluscs feed by straining tiny creatures and other **edible** matter from sea water. They take the water into their shell and over their **gills**. Bits of food are trapped in the mollusc's slimy **mucus**, and the pea crab helps itself whenever it is hungry.

I DIDN'T KNOW THAT

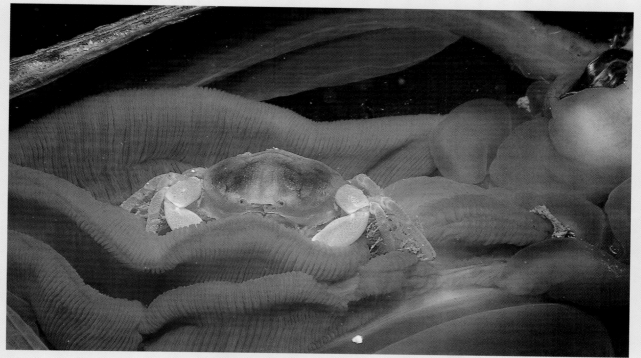

Threats and enemies

Crabs have many natural enemies. There are plenty of **predatory** animals that will catch and eat them. These include seabirds, otters, raccoons, wild cats and foxes (especially the crab-eating fox of eastern South America). Humans also enjoy eating crabs. For many people all around the world, crabs are a special treat. For others, they are a valuable source of **nutrition**.

Unfortunately, just like many other sea animals that people enjoy eating, some kinds of large crabs are in danger from **overfishing**. Although female crabs lay truly

Large numbers of valuable crabs, like these Dungeness crabs in the USA, are taken by fishing every year.

 Some species of crab live for only one year.

 The edible crab may live as long as twenty years.

 Detergents used in the 1960s to clean up oil spills at sea caused some crabs to lose their legs.

A sea otter on the coast of North America swims on its back as it cracks open a crab to get at the nutritious flesh inside.

enormous numbers of eggs, most of the **larval** crabs and tiny young crabs are eaten by hungry predators. The **edible** and Dungeness crabs reproduce before they are fully grown, but these smaller crabs still face more dangers than their fully grown relatives. It may take many years for them to reach full size, so if too many are taken by crab fishing, the remaining population may fall to a dangerously low level, threatening the **species**' survival.

Another threat, especially to the kinds of crabs that live in estuaries (river mouths) and along shallow coasts, comes from **pollution**. **Sewage** from towns near the coast is often allowed to flow into the sea. Although this can be nutritious for crabs, it makes them unsafe to eat.

Farming and other industries also spill some of their waste products into rivers and the sea. This causes changes to the water quality. Often they also introduce poisonous **chemicals** into streams, rivers, lakes and seas.

CRAB FISHING

Crabs are caught in the sea by trapping or netting. Crab traps are like baskets with an entrance that is easy for the crabs to walk into but from which it is not easy for the crab to escape.

These traps are **baited** with fish heads or chicken parts. Different kinds of crabs are taken, such as the **edible** crab in European waters and the Dungeness crab along the western coast of the USA. Nets are used to catch swimming crabs in south-east Asian seas, and Japanese and Russian fishermen also use tangle nets to catch king crabs and tanner crabs. The blue crab from the eastern coast of the USA is the most widely caught soft-shelled crab. These crabs are caught and eaten shortly after **moulting**, before their new **cuticle** has hardened. Because **overfishing** threatens the survival of this **species**, laws have been introduced in many places making it illegal to catch blue crabs under a certain size. It is also illegal to capture and keep a female blue crab carrying her eggs.

HUNGRY PREDATORS

In the sea, fish and octopuses feed greedily on crabs. Along the shore and in rock pools, seagulls and crows hunt for them. Land crabs are eaten by many **mammals**, especially foxes and raccoons,

A collared kingfisher from Indonesia is just one of many kinds of birds that regularly catch and eat crabs, and feed them to their chicks.

but in fact most animals will eat land crabs if given the chance. Around the shores of Scotland, otters catch crabs living among the seaweed, pulling them out of the water on to open rocks before cracking their shells with their teeth and eating the flesh.

A crab's hard shell is no defence against a hungry giant octopus. The octopus cracks open the shell with its hard, beak-like mouthparts.

In Africa, the giant water shrew is very fond of crabs and may eat as many as 25 freshwater crabs in one night.

Pollution

When gigantic oil tankers get wrecked on rocks or damaged by storms, enormous amounts of oil may pour into the sea. In a major oil spill, such as the *Exxon Valdez* disaster of 1989 in Alaska, people's first worries are for those birds that are so clearly harmed or killed by the oil.

The exact effect such a spill has on shellfish and **crustaceans** is often not known, but it is certain that these disasters can kill large numbers of crabs of many different species.

Unwanted Aliens

In any environment (place where things live), there is a balance among the animals that live there. It is not a good idea to introduce new **species** into an environment because it can upset this balance.

For instance, the green crab is naturally found near the **shorelines** of western and southern Europe but it has been introduced to North American shores, where it competes with the native Dungeness crab, both by eating its

The green crab is part of a balanced environment where it is found in Europe, but it is seriously affecting the populations of Dungeness crabs in its adopted North American home.

prey and by eating the Dungeness crab itself. It is also affecting clam, oyster and crab **fisheries**.

The Chinese mitten crab was an accidental introduction to the River Thames in the UK. People are worried that if its new home suits it, the burrows it makes will damage the riverbanks.

Glossary

abdomen part of an animal that usually contains the intestines, reproductive and other organs, but which in true crabs, is a thin flap folded against the underside of the thorax

anemone sea creature that sticks to hard surfaces. It has clusters of flower-like tentacles around its mouth.

antennae sensitive feelers that a crab uses to detect smells and to feel objects

arthropod invertebrate animal that has a tough outer layer and jointed legs

bait something used to attract and catch an animal

carapace hard shell covering the crab's head and thorax

carnivore animal that eats the flesh (meat) of other animals

chelipeds first pair of legs on a crab's thorax, each of which has a pair of pincers, or claws

chemical specific substance. Chemicals can be solids, liquids or gases in the air.

crevice narrow opening in a rock

crustacean group of arthropod animals such as crabs, lobsters, shrimps and barnacles

cuticle tough outer layer, or exoskeleton, of an arthropod that supports and protects the body inside it

debris scattered rubbish or remains

detect discover

edible fit to eat

exoskeleton hard outer layer that covers all arthropods

fishery business that breeds fish, crabs and other water creatures for food

gills organ that takes in oxygen from sea water, allowing crabs, fish and some other animals to breathe

identify recognize

invertebrate animal that does not have a backbone

larva stage in the life cycle of an animal that hatches from an egg, but which does not look like, or have the same structure as, its adult parents

mammal animal that is warm-blooded and feeds its young on milk

mate (verb) joining together of a male and female to produce young (offspring)

mate (noun) one of a male and female pair that have joined together to produce young

molluscs invertebrate animals such as slugs, snails, mussels, clams and oysters

moult shed the entire outer layer of skin or cuticle

mucus slimy substance made and given off by animals

nutritious describes food that helps an animal's body to work well

omnivore animal that eats plants and animals

overfishing when a sea creature is fished in such large quantities that the survival of that species in a particular area becomes endangered

oxygen colourless, tasteless gas in the air we breathe. All animals need oxygen to stay alive.

pincers pairs of claws that pinch, grip or cut

pollution damage to the environment caused by harmful substances and waste or rubbish

predator animal that hunts another animal for food

prey animal that is caught and eaten by another animal

protein substance containing carbon, hydrogen, oxygen and nitrogen that is part of all living things

reef ridge of rock or coral just under the surface of the sea

scavenge find food by searching among dead or decaying matter, either animal or plant

sewage human waste

shoreline part of the land where it meets the sea

species kind or type of living thing

territory area that an animal lives in and defends against others of its own kind

thorax part of the body between the head and abdomen

tidal mudflats muddy coastal land, covered by the sea at high tide

tide movement of the sea – towards and away from the shore. At high tide, when the sea comes in, the shoreline is covered in water. At low tide, when the sea goes out, the shore is uncovered.

tropical describes the hot regions near the equator

typical having features similar to others of its kind

vibration quivering or trembling movement of the air or ground

Further information

Books

Discovering Crabs and Lobsters, Jill Bailey (Hodder Wayland, 1987)

Life in a Rock Pool, Clare Oliver (Evans Brothers, 2002)

Looking at Minibeasts: Crabs and Other Crustaceans, Sally Morgan (Belitha Press, 2001)

Websites

www.enchantedlearning.com : search for 'crabs'

www.yahooligans.com : search for 'crabs'

Disclaimer
All the Internet addresses (URLs) given in this book were valid at the time of going to press. However, due to the dynamic nature of the Internet, some addresses may have changed, or sites may have ceased to exist since publication. While the author and publishers regret any inconvenience this may cause readers, no responsibility for any such changes can be accepted by either the author or the publishers.

Index

Numbers in *italic* indicate pictures

Titles in the Secret World of series include:

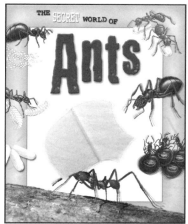

Hardback   1 844 21583 0

Hardback   1 844 21584 9

Hardback   1 844 21588 1

Hardback   1 844 21585 7

Hardback   1 844 21589 X

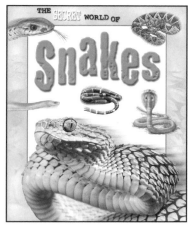

Hardback   1 844 21590 3

Hardback   1 844 21586 5

Hardback   1 844 21591 1

Find out about the other titles in this series on our website www.raintreepublishers.co.uk